Growth Marketing Operations, A Manual

Free Growth Marketing Ops Course:
https://www.udemy.com/course/draft/2623338

STRATEGY

Recapturing Marketing

The Fundamental Misunderstanding

Let's Talk About Ad Fraud

The Nightmare of Digital Marketing

TACTICS

Finding High-Intent Audiences

Marketing Technology Stack

Building Social Community

Producing Social Media Show

Creating Prospect List

Setting Up an SEO Blog

Choosing Tech Vendors

Integrating Marketing Technology

Recapturing Marketing

Some would say the goal of marketing has always been to generate new customers and bring back existing customers for more business. But in the era of Legacy Media, it was impossible to know when your marketing was seen and heard. This has traditionally meant that the role of marketing has been to sit down, shut up, and focus on salespeople, so to speak. But now, with digital media being as prevalent as it is, marketing technology options have exploded.

This puts the IT department and the marketing department at odds in many offices. IT is tasked with deploying software, while marketers develop specific workflows that can be significantly expedited by software. Consequently, the modern brand has found itself grappling with several stacks of technologies that support various aspects of the business. This new one, the marketing technology stack, lacks the best practices and ubiquity that other software industries benefit from.

Suddenly, the modern marketing specialist is drowning in a sea of vendors and data points, while having to operate marketing technology stacks that are a mixture of legacy software and arbitrary new software to fill gaps in a firm's repertoire. I promise you that no two marketing stacks are the same, nor are most marketing stacks operating efficiently, due to the lack of standardized practices across the industry as a whole.

It further complicates issues that the marketing process touches every other department in the business and so must work within their constraints while also regarding their goals. The Legal Department decides what can or cannot be said on the company website, IT sets the standards for required security, and Sales must generate a certain number of leads from specific geographic regions. Meanwhile, you can only market that which the operations teams have had the bandwidth to create and fulfill.

The marketing leader often fulfills many of the obligations and functions of an executive, despite legal risks and lacking the authority on paper. This clearly has pros and cons, but can lead to an ideal outcome so long as the CEO values and coordinates with the marketing leader in a unique way. For example, when the marketing leader announces that only one of the six proposed slogans were selected as satisfactory, it should signal something to the rest of the business. Likewise, when ten product descriptions have been implemented in the company's marketing initiatives but only two generate significant revenue, it should influence the way the company thinks about the entire culture of its sales operations.

A business will struggle to attain market success if there are misalignments between the product and the market. Misalignments of this nature undermine the opportunity for incremental product improvements.

To avoid this misalignment, the marketing technology stack of 2020 will need to integrate with every single piece of technology the firm operates on to capture everything that's happening as well as provide insight into the who, what, when, where, and why of its happening. It will be able to know where all your customers are coming from, what they're buying, and ultimately how much profit you made on that sale. This will require you to provide access to all of your Enterprise's data, and so we'll have to coordinate with all departments, and tap into every department's system of record.

The new rule of marketing will be the navigation systems of the ship that is their Enterprise. There will still need to be a person who plots the course forward, but there must also be a person directly behind them that tells the captain how the new waters are affecting the ship and which of the proposed paths forward can predictably bear fruit.

The Fundamental Misunderstanding

I'm no advertising industry veteran. I haven't exited a business north of six figures. I am, however, a classically-educated physicist, and I frequently use the same set of problem-solving skills in business as I do in physics problems. My foray into digital marketing was completely out of necessity.I wanted to make money (well, by selling the book I had just written--but success was clearly proportional to how many books I could sell).

It was only after spending two grueling months pulling everything I knew about DIY commercial aquaponics into a giant 150-page PDF, that I began to think about how to sell it. While everything I was learning from gurus and training programs focused on conversion marketing, I had no advertising budget to devote to the traffic needed to convert into sales. This resulted in several things simultaneously, which I will try to lay out in this chapter.

First, I made nine times as many sales of my hundred dollar book on Amazon than I ever did on my own SEO-rich websites and landing pages. While the results of every free case study I found by successful internet marketers, those people who I previously described as living lavish lifestyles funded by their clear understanding of how to make sales using the internet, whose results were always many times above benchmark results, the ad industry never took these people seriously

When I created those similar results for myself I began to wonder, "Why am I so above benchmark?" The average click-through rate cost per thousand Impressions, and cost-per-click is published for every known advertisement platform. For very popular social media platforms, these metrics are dissected even further into industry verticals, times of day, and age group by geography.

When I began to think about it, it dawned on me: a data set this large is highly indicative of what's going on in the big picture. This data has been collected for too long across too many disparate groups to be dismissed. So, when you start to see the work of digital agencies whose Marky(?) clients are so well-established in their markets, you can put two and two together. The ass-backwards approach of the giant Legacy ad agencies is driving down the global benchmarks for all digital marketing metrics.

Legacy ad agencies consistently achieve poor results because they don't understand how the internet actually works. They then find themselves in a position where they must allocate more resources towards ad budgets to generate enough engagement to succeed with their clients. I could go on forever with examples, but suffice it to say that you have seen plenty of ads of well-known brands that we have clicked on zero times. You know the kind of ad I'm talking about--the cringey "on brand" internet messaging that stinks like a skunk.

One of the main contributors to poor performance on all social media platforms by major ad agencies is a lack of nuance in their understanding of social media user psychology. The one term here you need to understand is the "network effect." It's how every major startup has reached the masses and thus large-scale operations. The network effect is when you have a certain number of users such that there is enough activity at all times on your platform so that any given new user feels like they are joining something already in play versus building a ghost town.

To reach this Holy Grail of benchmarks in a startup, you have to be truly focused on the user experience and working out the kinks in the activities that your users want to participate in. To increase user engagement, you often focus on an initial use case, a specific demographic that has been drawn to your platform. From there you incrementally build feature sets that maintain the core audience's engagement while bringing in new users, use cases, and eventually monetization options.

This all means one simple thing to marketers: The single reason social media platforms exist is to satisfy the needs of their core users' psychologies. This is the reason why each social media platform resides along all others in the marketplace and not on one singular platform that is used over all others. They're differentiated by their user's psychology, and thus anything that is advertised which does not match that expectation experiences low to normal levels of engagement.

When we, as marketers, speak the native language of each social media platform individually, we get better results. One could say that ultimately, when we speak the native language of the internet itself, that's when we achieve our highest engagement rates. Platform native language is authentic and simply impossible to fake. However, knowing the average user habit for every platform allows us as marketers to fine-tune our messages that much faster.

By matching the medium with the message, you are able to jump ahead to the top 10% of strategies and spend the rest of your time exploring your general product Market fit, versus being wildly incorrect and running out of ad spend. Recall that, depending on your resources and the ambition of your marketing goals, being 90% accurate is often enough. However, if you want the exponential gains of nearing 100% accuracy (which is only possible in theory) or you want to deeply understand one aspect of your digital journey for other business purposes.

We now have a situation where some of the most advanced advertising technologies are predicated on the idea that one message can be broadcasted across several different digital mediums; while we have an endless fight against ad fraud bots engaging in programmatic advertising processes. In digital marketing, you quickly realize how easy it is to be wrong and how difficult it is to be even *somewhat* right.

The first step in any digital research is often the thought experiment whereby you think of who your target audience is and where you can find them online at a reasonable cost (as compared to the average lifetime value for any given customer of yours). Once you know where you can target your ideal audience cost-effectively, you can then look to see what the native content format for that channel is and set out, after validation, to create a "social media show" for that platform specifically.

The goal of every social media show will ultimately be to provide genuine value to your prospective customers, at scale, from the very beginning of their digital customer journey. This often translates to FAQ type information, or "101" level knowledge of your industry, and Q&As packaged in the format for the medium you're targeting.

This marketing philosophy is colloquially known as "teach first, sell last." Due to the very low cost of production and distribution for such digital content, digital audiences have a great variety of alternatives and the cost to switch platforms is almost free. So not only can you not pitch at the top of your content, you don't need to because the cost of production is so low you can generate content and reach your audience at scale on a consistent basis. Remember: production value is inversely proportional to social media content success while quality of information is directly proportional to the engagement of such media.

Once you know who you want to target, and where they live online, you produce content for that specific combination. So if you can reach your buyers at scale cost effectively on YouTube, you make a DIY show. If they are on Twitter, you do a live Q&A regularly at a pre-scheduled time every week. If they're to be found on Facebook then you generate long-form informative blog posts.

"Who is my target audience? Where are they online? What is the native format of those online platforms?" Asking yourself these three questions will get you to the top one-half of digital marketers. Now after you do that comes a quick session of testing. The goal of this test is to produce your own high-value, in-house content for the long goal. You want to know you're making the right content before you invest, so a simple round of testing is crucial.

Two parts of testing for your own social media initiative are as follows: First, take everything you currently have and advertise it to every audience you can think of that is also identifiable on your platform. Whatever platform you're trying to test on, first Google if there are advertisement testing tools for that platform. As the rate of ad-tech and martech proliferation continues, there are likely new tools every quarter.

Ultimately, you're trying to find out who is engaging in what tab of benchmark levels. You want to know the benchmark click-through rate of the industry you're in for the social media platform that you are using. It will be one simple number to memorize going forward. However, if you want to be thorough then you should also note the average cost-per-click. This number, otherwise known as your click-through rate, is the single most important factor for any digital advertisement. This is because the only metric that actually matters at the end of the day is your return on ad spend per campaign.

This metric is often slow to become clear, requires a lot of different technologies to be integrated, and demands different departments to work hand-in-hand. In most startup circles, the customer acquisition cost is a key metric. However, this cost is often calculated retroactively. For the same reasons the return on ad-spend is difficult to ascertain, revenues take time to solidify and become accounted for through many channels. Keeping track of all of these factors requires Enterprise-level business intelligence that is very difficult to demonstrate in real-life contexts.

Consequently, the customer acquisition cost and your cost-per-lead have high value to business leaders. Everyone responsible for operating a company understands that the most they can invest in a customer before it becomes unprofitable. Therefore, every marketer tends to know what a sales lead is worth to the other departments.

As I stated earlier, the cost for generating leads is actually broken down into the cost for marketing lead and ultimately the cost-per-sale lead. Because we as marketers cannot often easily change nor optimize sales practices we must focus on what we can completely control. That is the cost/marketing lead, which is ultimately the contact information and permission to market-buy a prospect.

The cost per marketing lead is ultimately a function of the conversion rate at every stage in your digital customer journey. This is why you should always know how many people are converting at each stage and how much it costs to launch each advertisement campaign.

This is why testing all your content early for high click-through rates is a powerful indicator of customer intent as we will discuss in other chapters. At this stage, remember this: you want to take all of your content and advertise it to the relevant audiences you can target on a social media site you think will return maximal scaled distribution. Then model the content themes of your social media show around those clusters of topics that resonated most in your previous testing.

Now that you know what you're selling and who you're selling to, the next step is to figure out the other half of the equation. If you know what you're selling, then create content that describes what it is you're selling and the common problems that people have before they come to purchase your product. Then take that content and advertise it on the social media platform. You do not need any expertise or much time. Simply go to a site like Fiverr or hire a social media coordinator and have them go get subcontractors you need. Early on you want to build on a generalist basis and only bring on domain experts (like a strategist, copywriter, graphic designer, etc) once you really know where you're going.

If you don't know what to sell but know who you're selling to, then find content that you think they like and advertise it to them, looking for above average click-through rates. If you can identify influencers in that target market, you can see what kind of content works best on their accounts and you can copy and paste those URLs into your account and test them if you wish. This is where good old-fashioned marketing magic comes in. You'll know what kinds of things your audience will like, but you can find products by systematically testing products against your audience through advertisements like this online.

Remember, it does not need to be an expensive process. In fact, $5 a day will get you enough information in 2-3 months guaranteed. This is because you do not need a lot of impressions to achieve statistically significant results. Think about it this way: If you were to print out your digital ad on a flyer and pass it out on a street corner with a lot of foot traffic, you could gain a lot of insight when you examine how many people took the flyer. If 10 in 1000 take it versus a hundred in a thousand, you have the difference between a 1% click-through rate and the 10% click-through rate. This represents the difference between average and off the chart results within digital marketing.

Five dollars gets you in front of a thousand would-be clickers on whatever social media platform you're testing on, and thus the click-through-rate with a thousand impressions is, for all intents and purposes, very significant in the business world. The key here is to be consistent for 1-3 months. If it's going terribly after an entire month after an entire month of testing you can probably give up and if you are not satisfied with the results after 60 individual tests and it's safe to say you probably have a negative result.

Because there are so many people across so many platforms on so many devices it's imperative to know where to start testing to ensure a positive return on ad spend. Think of the surface of your Market like the surface of the Earth, and you're looking for these islands in the middle of the ocean. Anything underwater is not where you want to be, however it's where most of the mountain is.

By understanding the native message for every major medium you will be able to land on the island in a sea of cold chaotic Waters. Then, instead of spending all your time searching for land, you can spend all your time searching for The Summit.

Let's Talk About Ad Fraud

Fraud in the advertisement industry is so prevalent that to not understand it is to not understand the advertisement industry. According to some researchers, anywhere between 10% and 30% of all ad budgets are fraudulently expensed. This is mostly due to unknowing advertisers paying for clicks, views, and impressions generated by fraudulent sources.

Most of this activity is perpetrated by computer software created specifically to impersonate a human visitor. Its ubiquitous implementation strikes straight to the heart of the advertising industry. Because it is so wildly profitable, with some estimates suggesting over 4,000% return on your investment, it appears that there is a very strong motive for investing in this type of fraud operation.

Here's how ad fraud works: A domain and URL are created while bots are hired to visit that domain, resulting in what appears to be a high amount of (human) traffic. Then, programmatic ads are pushed out across that domain from known actors such as Google, Facebook, and Microsoft. Another set of bots can then be hired to come in and click on those ads - ads that were professionally created.

It's the ad traffic that is being faked to varying degrees of sophistication. With tens of billions of dollars being fraudulently collected by fake ad operations, this represents a massive problem for the digital economy. If the major advantage and promise of digital marketing is exact targeting, then knowing with certainty that successful targeting was in fact actually due to human interaction is key.

It appears that anything purchased through programmatic advertising auctions is rife with fraudulent metrics as to make it and possibly beneficial from a business standpoint. For this reason, I would suggest avoiding it at all costs. You can ask your advertising agency the following: "what has been your historic return on ad spend through purely programmatic acquisition channels?" The answer might be very uncomfortable.

Not every advertising agency will tell you that they deploy the latest software specifically designed to detect and filter ad fraud, or that such software is deployed at every stage of the digital advertising chain of supply. But it is. Yet ad fraud still runs rampant.

Even so, you would imagine that tech giants would nip this in the bud through their engineering prowess and endless resources, but they seem unable to stop it. The real problem is twofold. They aren't incentivized to actually stop this because a) the more volume of ads they sell the more money they make b) the more ad products they sell the more money they make.

So when it comes to programmatic ad-buying, it's such a cash cow for them that they dare not break it by instilling such a strict requirement as quality control. The good news is that there are several win-win solutions emerging; one focusing on technology underlined programmatic ad-buying while another focuses on the strategies involved in conversion marketing.

Since we're not here to develop a new technology, I'm going to focus on the strategies you can use today to minimize your exposure to ad fraud. It's really quite simple. Your entire marketing process can be broken into two pieces--the first being collection of marketing leads, and the second being conversion of those leads into sales leads.

The first step is defined by the collection of marketing information from the prospect and thus their permission for you to reach out to them. This is called consent-based marketing, or lead generation marketing, but I place it under the larger umbrella of conversion marketing. By collecting a prospect of buyers' contact information you are separating the wheat from the chaff. Now, in theory, more sophisticated bots could simply fill out this information, as you have probably seen in the comment section of any blog you've ever managed. But the next phase of your marketing system should diminish this tremendously.

The second piece of your marketing system should be to convert these marketing leads into sales leads. So once you have permission to contact your prospect through email, phone, SMS text, or what-have-you, your goal can then be to focus on educating and informing them about your product or service. This way, when they are ready to purchase they schedule a sales call with you (in the B2B space) or visit your sales page (in a B2C space).

The framework I've created helps you quickly identify the tasks you need to focus on to create these high-quality outcomes without prior knowledge. We'll get to it in later chapters, but for now it's important for you to understand why this has all been arranged the way it has. Because you are not looking to find new shores and calm seas, which is hard enough, your budget is constantly being ransacked by a thousand tiny fees.

By focusing your analytics and metrics of success around key performance indicators that reveal the achieved quantity of conversions, you can continuously optimize for real leads and not metrics created by Bots. The goal of marketing should be to create sales leads for your team, and with ad fraud being so prevalent you must MUST ignore vanity metrics. Because in this day and age you simply don't know which piece of engagement is a bot or not, unless they buy.

The Current Nightmare

There is not one marketing leader in the world today that feels completely comfortable in their marketing efforts. In fact, "discomfort" is not even the correct word. The current noise in digital marketing is more akin to the daunting and ominous task of looking for other life in the universe. Except that your business and livelihood depends on it.

While every ad vendor attempts to sell marketing leaders a myriad of products, only a handful work on any given platform. These handful of products that actually move the marketing needle tend to be the first few products the platform ever created. In other words, everything else is a sales tactic meant to increase market share and revenues.

When you calculate the number of combinations between platform and tech, it quickly becomes impossible to try them all. There simply is not enough money in the world to run enough ads in all the different places and in all the different formats to finally once and for all know what will work for your business.

And guess who has zero incentive to change that: everyone selling you ads! The more you buy the more everyone makes--end of story. So because of their legacy business model, marketing leaders are getting enlessles screwed. Well you might ask,

"What about all the ad metrics they show? What about all the clicks and impressions we're getting? Why is no one buying through these endless campaigns?"

The answer is simply because there is so much ad fraud out there. Russian bots are clicking on your ad placement ad infinitum making it impossible to understand who is truly clicking and why. That is, until you focus on conversion marketing and you throw out and destroy any semblance of importance one might place on vanity metrics.

The only digital metric that matters--ever--is your cost-per-lead. It does not matter if anyone watches or consumes your digital content if they are not interested prospects. If they're interested, many will move forward at least one step towards the point of purchase.

So if you are getting likes and comments but the ad seller is not converting any of those likes and comments into marketing leads, you have no idea if any of these people care about your product or service. This is why cost-per-lead is the only metric you should ever measure because it is made of the total conversion rate of the entire digital customer journey.

If your content fails to resonate with your prospect of audience, then your cost-per-lead may as well be infinite because your conversion rate across the entire funnel is zero. So, whenever anyone talks to you about engagement that doesn't convert directly into marketing leads, then they are either misleading you or are misled and mistaken themselves. In any case, they should not be touching your ad budget.

One's ad budget is one's oxygen--or, more accurately, it's your jet fuel. It does not matter how nice your engine is, how many people built it, or how many amazing things it can do if you don't have enough jet fuel to operate it. So be very cautious of people that want to spend your ad budget.

In the nightmare that is modern digital marketing you might be wondering where the solutions are, or the people who know what they're doing and can propose solutions at all. It's quite simple: most people that know what they're doing simply do it for themselves and have amazing lives. Conversion marketers almost always have their own lifestyle businesses that they automate and optimize for the type of Lifestyle they want. In doing so, they save themselves from working in the political nightmare that is the modern Ad Agency.

These conversion marketing truths are all over the internet. There are all sorts of tools and training and communities available to learn from but they're not suited for high growth startup culture or Enterprise scale culture. Most of these ad agencies are charging an arm and a leg while patting themselves on the back in their conferences. Meanwhile, they're focused on selling stuff that has nothing to do with digital marketing.

Nobody buys a car from a major manufacturer through their website. Now, there are a few startups selling cars through the internet but guess what tactics they're using: conversion marketing. The big agencies' legacy revenue models depend on brand marketing. This is why they show the customer base their client's logo as many times as possible in a single sales cycle. The iron with which they attempt to brand a client's logo onto your brain is heated by emotionally charged stories.

When you visit an established offline sales and distribution channel, like a grocery store, a mall, or an eleCTRonics store, you choose their client's product over the competitor. This is what it means to be branded as an X brand company versus a Y brand. You're still traversing the same waters most of the time.

Because the legacy advertising industry runs off of brand marketing retainers, none of their advice should be listened to when it comes to the digital aspects of marketing. Here's why: brand marketing is the antithesis to conversion marketing. While they work together in a modern marketing team they need to be positioned differently than they are today.

Brand marketing arose in a world where marketers had captive audiences. You were stuck sitting through TV shows regardless of the ads, you were going to flip through that magazine regardless of the ads, and you were going to listen to the radio station regardless of the ads. You had to experience those ads. You had no choice. Because you're unlikely to throw a magazine down in exchange for another one because of an ad, or change the TV or radio station because of an ad, you're captive to the message of the ad.

Advertisers could tell you whatever they wanted to and you had to consume it. Now their goal is to brand you with their client's product, so they spent their time trying to do just that. But the internet came along and made changing my YouTube video or fast-forwarding through a podcast or scrolling through my Facebook feed past all the ads virtually effortless! In fact, the user interface encourages me to do just that so that I can find what I want faster and stay there for longer on the platform.

The internet has been around for over 25 years and has reached maturity in a certain sense. We know what works and we know what doesn't, and it's rather ubiquitous for a large portion of the world. Now over those 25 years trillions upon trillions of data points have been collected regarding people's interactions with the internet. If you go and study the findings of enough successful marketing campaigns then you may notice a couple of trends.

Conversion marketing is all about iteration and continuous Improvement. It is about manufacturing. It is a science, not an art form like brand marketing. It is so cheap for me to get my videos in front of anybody on the internet that I want to stretch my ad budget very far. Since digital audiences are seeking quality of content, as opposed to quality of production, the cost for me to produce new content is much cheaper than legacy media. Because of the low cost of digital media production and distribution I can take the budget of a single 30 second TV spot for a car manufacturer and turn that into a year's worth of high-quality long form video content.

More importantly, if my analytics and attribution is set up properly, I can simply see who watches what and base my inferences on those observable parameters. This way, every time I put out new content it's made better by all the advertisements of previous content. This brings us to a fundamental axiom of conversion marketing--that a pay-per-click ad is the most honest form of customer feedback that you will ever get. This is because no one is forced to click on an app and if they do it is because they wanted to. So the imagery, copy, placement, and targeting of the ad is highly meaningful.

If you take this ethos to its logical conclusion, it means that in general when you launch 10 different ads to the same audience, those that perform at above benchmark for click-through-rate offer a deep insight into your audience's sales psychology. Because you can repeat this process at scale very rapidly, you're guaranteed to find what it is that, say, Auntie Anne cares about and why it is so valuable. Then you are guaranteed that your content marketing will elicit satisfactory conversion rates, given enough time.

With a good marketing stack you can do so much. The quality of a single piece of content is irrelevant because more likely than not your first one will suck and you'll have to keep trying until you get your brand's voice--the tone, targeting, content and theme--tighter and tighter.

Understanding how a good marketing technology stack is layered, integrated, operated, and optimized is 99% of modern marketing today. The rest is managing people's diverse array of personalities. Quality content is guaranteed to be produced, and ad budget maximized. There are so many other amazing benefits, one of which being that you get this market feedback rapidly and objectively. This kind of constant testing has implications for the rest of the organization because you're truly revealing the motivations and machinations of your market.

What we have at Vidulant is the step-by-step process for building the right marketing stack and the framework to understand immediately what kind of content should be made and where it should be placed. From Step 1, you can narrow your options down 10% that you can systematically explore so that you can get a very tight product Market fit in a very reasonable time frame and using a very modest budget.

The Vidulant process will transform media and advertisement because it'll allow for any brand to communicate with prospects faster, more affordably and effectively than ever before. That's why this field manual is so important. You must understand your "jet engine" for your brand which will be different for your market compared to other markets. When you understand how to build a jet engine--how and why they work--you can fix them quickly because you know what is required.

Finally, once you've put into place the processes for quality content creation on your own jet engine, the sky's the limit!

Why The Funnel Is Dead And Useless

Listen, when you and I were first learning how to sell, the math was simple:

See X number of people and Y will convert, because we know there's an average "conversion rate of" Z%.

Of course, you had to have a proven product and process. That's why franchises are still so popular. It takes money to find out what sells and why--a requirement to actually make a sale in the first place. Those of you who don't have one or both of those key facts, you live in a very different world of business development; a world that ends when you pass off a client as a salesperson.

For us salespeople, the "who" and "why" is the most important information we can get. The product is almost last. With a Vidulant Marketing Stack, you can find out both of those facts faster and cheaper than ever before. The power comes from a few major insights that have led to a revolutionary marketing automation software with incredible results.

All those benefits, however, stemmed from a single insight I had many years ago.

I was trying to explain what I do for people, to put on some marketing collateral, and was trying to illustrate how it's different- always a key selling point. The key was this: in digital marketing, the term "sales funnel" comes from the old days of sales; pitch X people, sell Y percentage. So when the first internet professionals were selling online, that was the way it was done.

When it worked, people didn't question it. However, back in the early days of the web (say, "Web 1.0"), there weren't as many webpages up- it simply cost too much to do because it was just too technical back then. So if you built it yourself, they would come. In those early days, you had traffic just because you existed! Your content was consumed because there was no competition:

In 1995 there were just over 25,000 websites.
In 2001 there were 17 million.
Today there are 1.3 BILLION.

So, if you had a funnel, you got traffic. It was that simple. If you had an offer, Y% would buy. But the internet was growing, changing, and maturing. Those who simply had "funnel" mentalities started seeing drops in sales. So, in 2000, Google turned on it's monetization strategy, a product called "AdWords." Suddenly everything changed. You could buy the keyword "wine" for $0.25. And a young man did just that, starting WineLibrary.com and growing it to a value of $30 million in a year (those of you who don't know Gary Vaynerchuck's story should look him up, he now runs a world leading social media agency).

So in 2000, there were 17 million websites but you could pay for instant, highly relevant, motivated traffic. As the number of websites on the internet continued to increase, so too did the overall user base, and thus began the bidding for keywords on platforms like Google AdWords. Smart marketers realized that you had to collect the email address of the person you just paid good money to click on your links. Best of all, once you had that contact information, you could reach out to that person for practically nothing, via email. And they'd open the email!

This is when the funnel began morphing into a jet engine; great marketers would squeeze all their paid traffic into a landing page, and build email lists. Then they'd sell everything they could to that email list to maximize their revenues. The compression, ignition, and channeling is the hallmark design of a jet engine.

But this model couldn't last forever. The proliferation of websites was directly linked to the drop in site publishing costs. As more people came online, they continued to gravitate around shared interests. Some of the very first webpages were chat rooms. This trend did not disappear. Soon came the "social media platform." Companies like Facebook took paid advertising to a new level. Soon, anyone could be reached via a paid ad, and the number of places they might see an ad grew as well.

Marketing technology software quickly became a mainstay in the digital marketing world. There were simply too many variables to track, and the customer experience of walking from one stage of the funnel into the next was quickly turning into a "multi-touch point customer journey" due to the growing number of competing distractions.

That's how the number of marketing technology solutions leapt from ~150 in 2011 to ~5,000 in 2017. Currently, most people are still trying to apply the long-dead "funnel" model to a completely new landscape. Feeling an ever-deepening drop in their return on ad spend, CMOs are getting fired if they can't compensate. However, all the solutions on the market do two main things (and neither works well): 1) they retarget like crazy, following people around with superfluous, ever-broadening discounts, and b) continuously increasing digital advertising budgets.

For instance, in the film industry, marketing budgets are ballooning as distractions mount and competition increases. Today, marketers have to spend an additional 50% of their movie's total budget just on marketing. It's becoming less and less effective, and thus the typical "superhero movies" become more prevalent--because, simply, they sell!

Nowadays, no one is coming to your website just because you put it online. No one. Zero. Further, meaningful organic traffic is going to take six months--at least--to generate. Luckily, you can buy targeted traffic and get relevant people to your site instantly. But it's not free, and attention spans are lower than ever. So you have to load your website up fast and get to the point immediately.

That's why those few people that come to your site and reach out or buy already made their decision before they ever visited. They did their research, they read the reviews, the found what they didn't want and then came to your site. This represents the smallest possible subsect of buyers (say 3%-5%) of the market who are ready and willing to buy. And that percentage is split between your entire market at any given time.

All while the 20% - 40% of buyers further out from the point of sale are just wandering around often making their decision based on whatever content they can find. This is why so many crappy products sell--because they were made by one of the few companies that set up their digital marketing right. They were simply the only ones at the table. So their product took a backseat to their presence.

In this rapidly expanding and heavily fractured market-space, the solutions of digital marketing are simply not keeping up. They're selling you their features, not the results. Much like advertising agencies (who say people will perform better than software), they don't know what they're doing and they don't care. No one does, so it's ok if any one vendor doesn't get the job done, there's a pervasive view that marketing (especially digital) is impossible and untraceable. That "1/2 of my marketing will still work, I just don't know which 1/2," is still a valid world view.

But that's just a lie. Anyone who tells you differently is either ignorant or lying. Today, you can track every click. But if you don't know what you're doing, selling online feels like a hunt for a needle in a haystack hunt for a needle in a haystack. Yet, for those who do, they make consistent and scalable sales. They grow companies like Mint.com and Zillow, without the need for a viral sensation like Facebook. They take a good product and get it in front of the right person with the right message.

They're called "growth marketiers" and they work with marketing technology stacks to find the lowest customer acquisition costs possible. The best ones, the few elite marketers, build Vidulant marketing stacks because they know that the optimal sequence- the average digital customer journey- has been proven to be standard through years of blind testing; the trillions of clicks, downloads, and purchases have shown a singular pattern.

Those few that follow this process will land in the top 10% of the market before they even start. Those at the top 1% will work to optimize their position from 90% to 99%- not from 0% to 50% (which probably takes roughly the same amount of energy).

Next, we'll break down the Vidulan'ts marketing process and MarStacks it creates.

Finding High-Intent Audiences

- ❏ Create digital customer persona:
    - ❏ Age: _____
    - ❏ Gender: _____
    - ❏ Keywords/Job Titles:_____
    _____

- ❏ Where are the top 3 platforms where you can find this audience online with good traffic and costs?
    - ❏

Platform	Traffic	Cost Per Click/View
Facebook		
Instagram		
Google		
Youtube		
Twitter		
LinkedIn		
Pinterest		

- ❏ Pick the best platform that has high-to-medium traffic and low-to-medium cost.

- ❏ What's the #1 best format for content on your top platform?
    - ❏

Platform	Native Content For Platform
Facebook	Blog Posts
Instagram	Personal Motivation
Google	Product Information
Youtube	DIY Video
Twitter	Q&A Conversations
LinkedIn	Career Training
Pinterest	Project Motivation

- ❏ Create ads on your #1 social media platform.
    - ❏ Target any audiences you can think of.
    - ❏ Send that traffic to the homepage of your brand/client.
    - ❏ Know your benchmark click-through-rate (CTR).
        - ❏ Search "[social platform in question] CTR benchmarks."

- ❏ Pick the most accurate industry and note its CTR:
  _____
- ❏ If nothing is accurate enough, use the average for the platform.
- ❏ Create a campaign and put all the information in the campaign name.
  - ❏ Like this: [brand initials] - [number of campaign] - [audience]_[offer]_[channel]
    - ❏ IE: "JEM - 1.2 - Training-Manual-YT"
  - ❏ Think of your ad-groups as a way to change your offer while still targeting the same audience.
  - ❏ Look for audiences+offer combinations that click-through-your ad at a higher than average CTR.
- ❏ The goal is to find the ads, targeting your customer audiences, that create the highest click-through-rates.
  - ❏ Save this headline as a "winningest" CPC ad:
    - ❏ Image:
      _____
    - ❏ Headline 1:
      _____
      _____

❏ Headline 2:
_____
_____

Marketing Technology Stack

Standard Marketing Stack:

Size Of Platform	Small	Medium
Ad Management Software	Ad Espresso	
Content Management Software	Webflow (B2C),	Hubspot (B2B)
Offer Management Software	Instapage	Leadpages
Communication Management Software	Mailchimp	
Attribution Management Software	Google Analytics	Google Marketing Platform

Custom Marketing Stack:
- ❏ Ad management Software:
- ❏ Content Management Software:
- ❏ Offer Management Software:
- ❏ Communication Management Software:
- ❏ Attribution Management Software:

Marketing Stack Checklist:
- ❏ Does every piece work, at a minimum?
- ❏ What pieces are converting above average?
- ❏ What pieces are converting below average?
- ❏ Who is in charge of every piece?
  - ❏ Ads:

- ❏ Content:
- ❏ Offers:
- ❏ Emails:
- ❏ Attribution:
- ❏ Is there a single dashboard that anyone can view to see the performance of your marketing stack?
- ❏ What is your cost-per-lead:
  - ❏ Per channel:
  - ❏ Per country:
  - ❏ Per Audience:

Building Social Community

- ❏ Does everyone understand the 80/20 content rules?
    - ❏ 80% From other sources
    - ❏ 20% Made in-house
- ❏ What are the top 9 pages/channels that your audience also follows on the top platform?
    - ❏ _____
        _____
        _____
        _____
        _____
        _____
        _____
        _____
        _____
    - ❏ Who is checking these weekly for content?
        _____
    - ❏ What kind of content calendar are you using?
        _____
- ❏ What kind of content will you be producing in-house?
    - ❏ (NOTE: if you make a video, you can repurpose it as audio+blog posts)
    - ❏ Blog Content:
        _____
    - ❏ Podcast: _____

- ❏ Video Show: _____

- ❏ What is the ad budget per content piece:
- ❏ What is the production budget per content piece:
- ❏ How often is someone checking for helpful content?
    - ❏ Crawl: Monthly
    - ❏ Walk: Weekly
    - ❏ Run: Daily
        - ❏ It's important to be relevant, so a daily effort to check sites for content is ideal.
- ❏ What kind of content calendar are you using?
    - ❏ Software:
    - ❏ Spreadsheet Template: (Recommended)
- ❏ Where is your content calendar located and does everyone who needs access has it?

Producing Social Media Show

- ❏ What is the name of your "Social Media Show:"
    - ❏ "Name Of Your Company" Show is perfectly acceptable.
- ❏ What platform will it be made for?
    - ❏ Who will be responsible for each part of the show?
    - ❏ Monitoring Social Media:
    - ❏ Answering Social Media Questions:
    - ❏ Filming/Recording Each Episode:
    - ❏ Editing Each Episode:
    - ❏ Uploading To Acquisition Channel:
    - ❏ Advertising On Each Episode:
- ❏ What is your production kit of parts?
    - ❏ Camera:
    - ❏ Microphone:
    - ❏ Tripod:
    - ❏ Lighting:
    - ❏ File Storage:
    - ❏ Location Of Kit:
    - ❏ Responsible For Kit:
- ❏ Who's needed for each episode?
    - ❏ Who's the host?
    - ❏ Where will you shoot?
    - ❏ Who's needed to shoot?
- ❏ What's the format of the show?
    - ❏ Customer Interviews
    - ❏ Team Interviews

- ❏ News Commentary
- ❏ How long will the show be (from easiest to hardest)?
    - ❏ 5 minutes
    - ❏ 15 minutes
    - ❏ 30 minutes
    - ❏ 60 minutes
- ❏ How often will you schedule your show (from easiest to hardest)?
    - ❏ Monthly
    - ❏ Weekly
    - ❏ Daily

Creating Prospect List

- First, we need to all agree on what the goal of this marketing list will be.
  - Finding New Customers
  - Reselling Existing Customers
  - Testing New Ideas
  - Selling A Specific Product/Service
  - Registering Attendees For A Physical/Digital Event
  - Establishing A Social Media Community
  - Finding High-Intent Audiences
  - Testing New Marketing Technology
- Do you have all the parts needed?
  - Proven Acquisition Channel
  - Landing Page Software
  - Email Management Software
  - Integration Between Landing Page & Email Softwares
  - Offer That Can Be Fulfilled With Internal Processes
  - Welcome Message That Fulfills Offer
- Who will manage the entire process?
- What internal people need to be pulled into a standing meeting?
- What's the planning document called and does everyone have access to it?
- Does the planning document have the benchmark CTR for your chosen channels?

- What new technologies are needed to ensure this can succeed?
    - Ad Management: just use the social media ad platform that you've identified as your main and thus first digital acquisition channel.
    - Content Management: all you need is a landing page software that can integrate with your email service provider. If there is any piece that you must get approval to use, this is the one. Even if you need to make custom landing pages for final use, testing new landing pages rapidly is the number 1 factor that will increase your odds of success.
    - Offer Management: again, a landing page tool, ultimately, is an offer management system.
    - Email Management: you don't need this piece to get started and build your list. It makes things better and faster, but in the interim, you can simply export your contacts from the landing page tool you use and email it to whomever manages your email marketing. Remember: it's a process, so get focus on iterating between process versions; first manually, then automatically.
    - Attribution Management: all you'll need to start is the stats in your

- landing page tool. Getting this data into a dashboard is a whole other program and will require its own focus.
- With the tools in place, we can now start deploying tactics.
- Create a campaign that targets your top "high-intent audience."
    - This process is all based on how well you can think like your audience, and how well you know your customer.
    - Your first goal is to understand what's most valuable and to whom.
    - Use your ad campaigns to separate experiment sets.
        - Use your brand's initial at the beginning of every campaign.
        - Track clusters of ad campaigns with a simple number: x.yz
            - 1.1, 1.2, 1.3.... 1.9, 1.91, 2.0
            - Use the first number to distinguish distinct phases in your learning.
            - 1.0 is all about general audience research.
            - 2.0 might be a more clearly focused track

- "How to start" vs "all" or "general"
- 3.0 might be coming back to the general market audience but with new learnings
    - "How to start" doesn't is full of junk traffic.
- Use the Market-Product-Fit framework to find increasingly better CTRs.
- Use the CTR metric to guide you to better and better market-product-fits.
    - Average Google + Landing Page conversion is = .08%
    - You should target a combined conversion rate of 0.16% or more.
        - This is your Marketing Lead Conversion Rate
        - = Ad Click Thru Rate * Landing Page Opt-in Rate
- If you do not have any sales email written (perhaps because you don't know what you're selling), here are your options:
    - Send nothing. But you'll have to consider those marketing leads that

did not get as cold once you do send them something.
- ❏ Send them 1 email, immediately. Here, you'll have to send them their offer for maximum effect.
- ❏ Send them blog posts weekly (aka a newsletter). This'll take about an hour a week.
- ❏ Send them blog posts daily. This will require about 3-6 hours, once a week.

Setting Up SEO Blog

- ❏ Who is the program leader:
    - ❏ Will it be a revolving role?
- ❏ Is there an existing website with hosting:
    - ❏ If yes, who is in charge of that:
        - ❏ Can they add a subdomain, "www.blog.yourwebsite.com?"
    - ❏ If no, what hosting service will you use: (my default is www.Dreamhost.com)
- ❏ Who will install your blog: (dreamhost.com has a "1-click install" feature)
- ❏ Who will manage the blog:
- ❏ Who will buy the theme:
    - ❏ Where will you buy your theme from: (my default is https://envato.com/)
    - ❏ Always start with a template:
        - ❏ Costs under $100
        - ❏ Built to modern SEO/UX standards
        - ❏ Often comes with support
- ❏ Does your theme meet all the minimum requirements:
    - ❏ Less than 1 year old
    - ❏ Single purpose
    - ❏ Single page
    - ❏ Mobile responsive
    - ❏ Load time is under 5s
- ❏ What are the top 5 themes you feel are on brand:

- [ ] 1
- [ ] 2
- [ ] 3
- [ ] 4
- [ ] 5
- [ ] Once installed, who needs admin access:
- [ ] Who needs contributor access:
- [ ] Where will you get regular contributors from:
    - [ ] Inhouse team member:
    - [ ] Freelancer Pool:
    - [ ] Independent Contractors:
    - [ ] Copywriter Service:
- [ ] Who will need to approve posts before they go live:
- [ ] What security plug in will you use: (my default is "All In One WP Security")
- [ ] What CDN plugin will you use: (my default is "Cloudflare")
- [ ] What internal blog ads will you use:
    - [ ] "Right Sidebar" inhouse ad:
    - [ ] "Post Content" inhouse ad:

Choosing Tech Vendors

- [ ] Is your core marketing stack working:
- [ ] What is the business goal of this new marketing technology:
    - [ ] Where does it fit into your existing stack:

- ❏ What technology does it need to integrate with your existing stack:

- ❏ What do crowd review sites suggest:

- ❏ What are the most advertised solutions:

- ❏ What is the SINGLE most important feature:

- ❏ Which vendors offer monthly pricing:

- ❏ Which vendors have more support than sales:

- ❏ Decision Matrix of vendors that have single most important feature:

Top 3 Vendors	Cost Per Month	Marketing/Sales

Integrating Marketing Technology

- ❏ Are there any known points of failure in your marketing stack?
- ❏ Does any piece of your stack not receive or send information adequately to any other?
- ❏ Where does the data come from?
- ❏ Where does the data need to go?
- ❏ What format does it come in as?

- ❏ What format does it need to leave as?

- ❏ Does zapier.com adequately integrate the 1 or more marketing technologies in question?
- ❏ What in-house team member or vendor could create a custom integration?
- ❏ Is there a planning document for this program?
- ❏ What quality assurance procedures must be used to test the integration?
- ❏ Does legal require input on custom integrations?

www.ingramcontent.com/pod-product-compliance
Lightning Source LLC
Chambersburg PA
CBHW021513210526
45463CB00002B/998